From
FATHERLESS
to
FATHERFUL

REE DEEMD

WESTBOW
PRESS®
A DIVISION OF THOMAS NELSON
& ZONDERVAN

This book is a work of non-fiction. Unless otherwise noted, the author and the publisher make no explicit guarantees as to the accuracy of the information contained in this book and in some cases, names of people and places have been altered to protect their privacy.

WestBow Press books may be ordered through booksellers or by contacting:

WestBow Press
A Division of Thomas Nelson & Zondervan
1663 Liberty Drive
Bloomington, IN 47403
www.westbowpress.com
844-714-3454

ISBN: 979-8-3850-0514-7 (sc)
ISBN: 979-8-3850-0515-4 (e)

Library of Congress Control Number: 2023915203

Print information available on the last page.

WestBow Press rev. date: 10/10/2023

FOREWORD

I want to first thank my Heavenly Father for awarding me this second life here on earth to live, learn, and share with you all.

The One who made Himself into a human because of the fall of our own personal choices and loved us to the point of death... while taking the place on the cross for our sins, He enabled a life for all to be reunited with Him in eternal life.

A pro bono gift, to last for eternity, this offering I will never cease to be thankful for, but also, for taking the place of a 'father' in my life and allowing me to go from 'fatherless to Fatherful'.

In a similar sense, I give thanks to my family and friends who have been gracious in various ways, but mostly in patience through this journey. Thank you for being such wonderful hosts throughout these years.

The select few that have done their parts to establish the confidence necessary to write this book, for seeing the good in me (when I didn't see it myself), and my children who show me in the physical form, the purity and unconditional love of Jesus daily. Forever grateful for these encounters and the impact you all have had on me in writing this book. I pray that I become a conduit as you once were, allowing the Holy Spirit to have His work fully throughout me.

TABLE OF CONTENTS

INTRODUCTION

Fatherless is something we are born into, arrive at, or discover during our lifetime. One can be "fatherless" even if a father is present, if he is an uncaring harsh, or antagonistic man. It resonates with many Americans, as well as international citizens and it impacts more than we know. This book is designed to take that label and transform it into something transformative, a discovery, and a relationship that is long lasting and fulfilling. I speak not as a theologian, but as a layman because that is exactly what I am; I pray that your critiques take that into consideration. By joining this trek, one can finally feel Fatherful, and eliminate their once known label.

Unlike the statement that "it doesn't happen overnight", Fatherful can be something that does, in fact, happen overnight, requiring minimal effort (the simple acceptance of God's gift of salvation). A manifestation of effort towards being the best version of oneself is most certainly continual...gratefully this is not done alone.

Be aware that you will make mistakes along the way, this does not make you a failure, forgiveness is offered through repentance. Keep your hiking shoes on and make friends along the way.

Reflection

At the end of each chapter, we will have a time for **Reflection**, a time for you to be open about your circumstances and your feelings, much like you haven't been allowed to do before in society.

You can take a deep breath of relief; God isn't like society. He wants you to be as transparent as possible, He wants to hear all facets of your pain and He wants to heal you from it.

I encourage you to seek and enroll in Godly counsel throughout this process. You can even bring the **Reflection**s of this book to assist in your encounters. I believe God uses each individual according to their gifts which He provides at salvation. (I will go into further detail about vetting counselors in the latter portion of this book as I think it's essential for continued growth). Counseling shouldn't be stigmatized; I have a Christian Counselor whom I will never fire, who seeks counsel from the Lord and others and then disseminates that to me. Instead, I believe that it should be stigmatized to <u>avoid</u> utilizing services of assistance based on the feelings and perceptions of others. We are all conduits in this life, specific to our innate gifts and we need other's skills to help our skills thrive[1].

Are you ready to begin the journey?

---

[1] 1 Corinthians 12:12-27, English Standard Version

Chapter 1
'FATHERLESS'

"He didn't want you."

$\mathcal{I}$ STILL REMEMBER THE DAY I asked her, holding my mom's hand as we walked back to our home from the local market. I could see a tall building on my left and a train track that went over an underpass straight ahead of me.

As my eyes focused on the scenery, my mind focused on something else…I had observed an absence that seemed to defy the normative family pictured on TV. I had to ask her about this absence, I felt as if a huge chunk of information had eluded me the first seven years of my life.

My mother was a tough parent, and purposefully… she was raising three children with no help. She did not allow any form of manipulative pressure, knew her own boundaries, and displayed to all her children that we weren't going to force her into anything.

Knowing this, I was frightened to ask. As I mustered up the strength, my hand pulsated and my lips tremored until finally, I received enough courage to speak…and just like that it slipped out….

"Mom who's my dad?". "I don't want to talk about it, Ree. He didn't want you".

Those words stung much harder than any bumblebee that I had

stepped on in the grass, with the same effects of the venom but much stronger and towards the heart. "He...didn't...want...you."

I'm sure she anticipated that moment, since my inception—the truth about the situation pained her to admit (the truth is still a bit obscure even now), but it did not come delivered like a nice piece of steak on a silver platter. For the next few years and well into adulthood I repeated those four words continuously. I visualized every individual I met as having a father who wanted them. Understandably, I grew unhappy about myself and my surroundings, I had everything essential to live but I did not have the vertebrae of my young female being...a physical father.

A Sanctified Definition

Webster's dictionary defines being fatherless as being without a living father or not having any association with a living father; 'related words' include friendless, parentless, leaderless, unprotected, aidless, and many more (n.d.).[2] This word also can be an adjective for the spiritually fatherless as well.

For the majority, when you're fatherless, you can:

- wander;
- search for meaning in individuals;
- find relations to fulfill the relation that you've lost;
- try to replace/create memories with new experiences;
- have an altered mental state;

When you're fatherless spiritually you often:

- wander without direction;
- find detrimental ways to support unfruitful connections;

---

[2] Merriam Webster Dictionary

- are absent of a leader beyond yourself;
- adventure through life by the skin of your teeth;
- are without aid;
- are without structure and discipline;
- are without true agape;

The definitions, in ways, are synonymous; fatherless: without a physical father, fatherless: without a spiritual Father, and in the same, both situations leave you hungry for something soul-satisfying.

When you're fatherless physically, there may be a higher chance of you being fatherless spiritually. It's hard for us to embrace this definition, like being on the lower tier of what we might assume a stratum; those who have it all together on the upper level, and us somewhere near the bottom. It's exhausting but important to recognize that if you have an absence of a paternal role in your life then you are in fact 'fatherless'.

Maybe the absence in your life is of one or the other (spiritual Father, physical father), or maybe it's both…but one thing's for certain if you're reading this book…something is telling you that the depths of your soul are hungry for more.

What is the solution to being famished? When we get hungry physically, we eat and are filled, right? But, as fatherless, it's not as if you can force someone to be your father. Imagine this illustration: "Excuse me sir! Please be my dad, I need filled I need satiated!". It doesn't work like that in this world, but in the spiritual sense, it certainly does (in a less aggressive way!) And God's cool with it, He knows you're hungry for fulfillment, He has been watching and waiting for you to finally say you're hungry. Kind of like a child that refuses to eat your meal because of a restriction you had against them…stubbornness…we all know Junior is hungry and he at some point needs food. We've been very stubborn in responding to our state of needing fulfillment, assuming that we could survive by ourselves…and we could…but is that the abundant life? The ideal life?

Our ideal life, our ideal self, that abundance comes because of submission to hunger. A submission to the One who has already been cooking for years waiting on you to take a sip of the broth. He's been your Father all along. The One who you may have never noticed or in your healing stages have been too distracted to notice.

The solution to that hunger, that pain, that sadness that you refuse to show to the world, that void that has been permeating all other areas of our life…that our inner being cries for, His name is Jesus. He is God, and God is Him. God essentially sent Himself in human form to alleviate everything you've been going through. To say, "Hold up…I know that hurts, let Me take it from you." Like a friend that takes the other end of the couch you're carrying, to help you move it to the other side of the room with greater ease.

Most importantly, being spiritually Fatherless means being subject to God's righteous judgement:

"..for all have sinned and fall short of the glory of God" (Romans 3:23, NIV)

"There is no one righteous, not even one" (Romans 3:10, NIV)

"For the wages of sin is death, but the gift of God is eternal life in Christ Jesus our Lord." (Romans 6:23, NIV)

The way to receive the gift, and become Fatherful, is outlined in John 3:16 (NIV) – **"For God so loved the world that he gave His one and only Son, that whoever believes in Him shall not perish but have eternal life."**

Further, Romans 10:13 (NIV) – **"Everyone who calls upon the name of the Lord shall be saved."**

God is available in all ways to feed the God-specific needs in our lives, and this, my friend, wasn't meant to be filled with anyone else but Him.

"Then they cried out to the Lord in their trouble,
and he delivered them from their distress.
⁷ He led them by a straight way

to a city where they could settle.
8 Let them give thanks to the Lord for his unfailing
love and his wonderful deeds for mankind,
9 for he satisfies the thirsty
and fills the hungry with good things."
(Psalm 107-6-10, New International Version)

<u>Reflection</u>

Have you noticed any similarities with the definition of fatherless in your experience? List them below.

_____

_____

_____

_____

_____

How about in the spiritual sense? List them below.

_____

_____

_____

_____

_____

_____

Have you ever heard of the concept of 'God the Father'? What did you assume this entailed?

_____

_____

_____

_____

_____

_____

_____

_____

Are you willing to allow God to assist in moving the couch?

_____

_____

_____

_____

_____

_____

_____

_____

_____

Chapter 2

FROM FATHERLESS
TO FATHER-FULL

*Filling your God-shaped void, with
nothing less than the Father.*

**"A Father to the fatherless, a defender of widows,
is God in His holy dwelling."** (Psalm 68:5, NIV)

𝓛OVE IS A HEFTY EMOTION that we most correlate with happiness. It is a feeling that we cannot seem to shake when we attain it, one that drives us mad and keeps us going back for more and more. During the eighties, a fellow by the name of Robert Palmer debuted a song called 'Addicted to Love'; this song won a Grammy award for record of the year, four MTV video awards, and has been covered by over six other artists. When you dive into the lyrics, you can understand why:

> *"It's closer to the truth to say you can't get enough
> You know you're gonna have to face it, you're addicted to love."*[3]

---

[3] Robert Palmer, *Addicted to Love.* The Island Def Jam Music Group, 1985.

Can you resonate with these lyrics, maybe say I feel you? A little louder for the people in the back?

Fast forward to 2023 and we can see the theme of that song (being addicted to love) coming to fruition. Although we claim that we can do things on our own, maybe that 'we don't need love', our personal lives may say otherwise. Through our involvement with a social media addiction, gaining likes through our posts, checking our apps to see if we have any messages, and becoming paid influencers...we all have this innate craving, to feel and be loved and cherished.

Reviewing this psychologically and biologically it's in our DNA. Simply put, all animal kingdoms need love from the lowest level to the highest functioning.

The first glimpse of love remembered has been received (in the best scenario) from our parent(s). As they birth us into this world, they too are filled with a love that only something of a higher power can deliver, unconditional and true agape[4].

As we need their sustenance to survive, we end up being obligated to be in their care. Usually, this is a benefit, and thus as a result lends to overflowing love.

As continuous exposure proves, we stimulate and develop personality traits and characteristics that make our sense of value and self-esteem secure and concrete.

Known to be our supreme attachment figures, our parents teach us how to potentially communicate, form relations, and handle conflict.

Without that paternal sense of direction, we may become unsure of who we are, we may wander around **addicted to** finding **love** in any capacity.

---

[4] "**agape**, Greek **agapē**, in the New Testament, the fatherly love of God for humans, as well as the human reciprocal love for God. In Scripture, the transcendent *agape* love is the highest form of love and is contrasted with *eros*, or erotic love, and *philia*, or brotherly love"
"Agape," Encyclopædia Britannica, https://www.britannica.com/topic/agape.

In a recent Facebook post, a video illustrated how a father had invested time in his daughter annually, taking her out to a restaurant so she could develop an understanding of how she should be treated had she been courted as an adult. This loving father dressed to the nines while her mother dressed her accordingly. He then ran a few errands and when it was time for their father-daughter date, he rang the doorbell, asked the mother for his daughter, took her hand, opened the door for her, and escorted her on their way. The daughter lit up with joy and amazement in this short segment, impressed with how her father made her feel that evening, this desirable feeling of being loved and cherished.

We can gawk at this beautiful act, marvel at his compassion, or we can claim it to be just for show. Ultimately though we can agree that this illustration visualizes how a father can affect a daughter. We know (by this and many other examples) how much power a parent, especially, a father, has over the psychological development of a child.

If the behavior in the home is consistent throughout the child's life, she will likely grow to be a young lady who settles for nothing less than what her father did for her. She will remember that her father always chose her; she will understand her worth.

Numerous studies have been conducted to verify this hypothesis and to understand the role of fathers in child development. Like others, a particular one concluded that if the perception of the involvement of a father was positive, then the self-esteem and life satisfaction of a child (daughter) were also positive.[5]

Regardless of this finding, unfair as it is, some of us were unfortunately not awarded the same likelihood, for one reason or another (death, divorce, illegitimacy, etc.) and we are left without the parental stability that most nuclear families receive.

---

[5] Gabriela Sebokova, "The Role of Father Involvement in Psychological Well-Being of University Students," *EDULEARN Proceedings*, 2018, https://doi.org/10.21125/edulearn.2018.1158.

Not surprisingly, we know that this lack of presence affects not only our idea of a family but our idea of ourselves. Trudging through the difficulties of life without a consistent, faithful father figure as an example of what we would expect a Heavenly Father to be, we find it more difficult than our normal counterparts to adjust, seemingly leaning on uneven soil again and again as we try to fill a hole, a longing in our hearts that can only be filled with a God-shaped key.

If you, like me, have been fatherless (in any sense…spiritually, physically, emotionally, or all at once) *I would like to apologize and sympathize with you on an interpersonal level and let you know it wasn't your fault. Nothing you could have done would have stopped this position that you find yourself in. But their absence does not affect your value, your worth…I may not know who you are, but I know that* **God** does.

Even in your aloneness, God was there. He has had His eye on you for quite some while, and He knows you're hurting…He's been with you in the furnace[6] despite it seeming like it had only been you.

He wants me to tell you that despite the circumstances, those of a negligent, absent, deceased, *(or one that made you feel like you weren't enough)* father, God has had a bigger plan for you.

He chose you to be His child, through the act of your faith in Christ, just as He chose me to reach out to you, He chose to love you in place of the void of your father. He chose you to inherit His kingdom as His heavenly heir. You are an heir of the King, and once you realize this, once you accept Him you will no longer be classified as '*fatherless*', but **<u>Fatherful!!</u>**

---

[6] Daniel, Chapter 3, English Standard Version.

Chapter 3
A GOD-SHAPED VOID

*F*OR A QUARTER CENTURY OF my life, I have gone through these adversities... the turmoil of being affected by being fatherless. The self-esteem highs, the lows, the addiction to love, the desert of loneliness, and the thoughts; have shaped me more than I'm proud of and have taken a toll on my upbringing.

I am thirty-one years old, and I still have not met my biological father. I have never seen a picture of him, never heard his voice, and have never been kissed on the forehead by any father figure. He didn't walk me down the aisle on my wedding day, he hasn't answered any "Dad, what do I do?" phone calls, and he hasn't funded me a single dollar toward a life without him.

Throughout life, this absence has affected my understanding of myself drastically, especially his lack of desire to remain in my life. Gratefully, however, a Man appeared in my life, a Man who made me tear apart all the pages of my history and burn them. He led me to start a new journey, one that allowed me to see myself through a new lens, one of security, value, and confidence...and to fulfill a mission in others of the same.

Likewise, He chose **you** as one of the same. None of His children are any more or less significant than you. Even those with the biological fathers, the Bugatti, the financial inheritances, and the intellect. Your value is the same as theirs.

He chose **you** and continues to choose you. You see you are absolutely essential to Him. He chose you to love you. He chose to sacrifice His only Son to die on the cross so you could escape your reality.

That role, the one that we've been longing to be filled by our earthly fathers, can be filled and never emptied again if we let it. Yep, it's that simple…It's not a magic trick, but it's certainly magical what becomes of the decision.

His Word tells us in many verses, that people fade away, they are merely temporal, and no one is meant to stay in our lives forever. I know this is disappointing, I really like my cat too. This wasn't the plan to begin with, He had meant prosperity and peace for us, a world where all things and beings lived in harmony…this was the plan God had for us. Sounds amazing, right?

However, an actual supervillain came along, the "opposer" (Satan), who aided in the fall of mankind, our perfect life, all those good intentions were turned against us through the fault of our ancestors.

What remained was God the Father, Jesus, His Son and the Holy Spirit, revealed to us through His Word, allowing you another chance (we will get more into this very shortly). The Spirit of the Lord will never leave you — when you invite Him in.

"All flesh is like grass, the grass withers but the word of God remains" (Isaiah 6:8, New International Version).

It's time to stop letting the hurt have that much hold over our lives. Let's get ready to let go, to stop jamming the keyhole with keys that are not engineered to fit, it's time to let a Conqueror, (the One who had our plan in place before our biological donors even contemplated it) fill the place; it's time to change our common identifier from father*less* to Father**ful**.

Reflection

What is your story about your father? Feel free to respect your own boundaries here but know that there is literally no one here to judge your experience. God already knows.

_____

_____

_____

_____

_____

_____

How has his absence affected you? Think back to childhood, to your personality, to the way you view relationships, your understanding of yourself, your confidence.

_____

_____

_____

_____

_____

_____

_____

How has your attitude been shaped because of his absence?

_____

_____

_____

_____

_____

_____

_____

How do you feel hearing that God is willing to replace that role in your life, to be your father? Are you uneasy, excited, nervous, afraid to mess it up?

_____

_____

_____

_____

_____

_____

_____

_____

Chapter 4
ACCEPTING THE TITLE 'FATHERLESS'

*T*HIS JOURNEY FOR YOU, ME, and many other individuals in this world has been a hard one. Seeing yourself in the mirror and reflecting on the memories you've spent with the newly lost parent, looking at your eyes and wondering what your fathers may have looked like, sitting across from your adopted parents who don't resemble you at all…those daily occurrences are awfully hard to swallow. It's true, it could have been someone else's life, but somehow it was yours… and that truth is even harder to fathom.

My brother is one of my mother's favorite children, which was apparent through her actions. She would make sure to make him happy with his favorite foods and desserts every time he visited.

Likewise, my brother and I had one of the strongest connections a sister and brother could have; Mom and I enjoyed his company more than anything in the world. On one occasion when he visited, I knew this was my chance to retrieve what I believed I needed. She had been avoiding the question all my life. I didn't want to hurt her, so I tread carefully.

As we sat there, the energy that once built me as a child resonated with me again. Within a few minutes, I randomly asked her, "Mom what is his name, my father's?". I was sixteen, with little to no knowledge of anything about him; not even my sister or brother (who were much older …we all had different fathers) knew. Instead of her usual hesitation and avoidance, she told me his name! She didn't know where he was…he never contacted her again and he didn't want children.

I thought I had the golden ticket. She had given me all the information I needed to know to make my life complete. Or supposedly. I could finally know who my other half was, where my genetics came from…what he looked like…I could finally be complete. But just as fast as that temporary excitement entered my heart, it quickly dwindled. Armed with his name, I scrolled the Internet yellow pages to find my father for what seemed like the millionth time. The trail of information stopped in the late nineties/ early two thousands, and nothing else could be found; my instinct told me he had moved, but my heart couldn't accept that.

Over the years I had seen so many people get kissed and hugged by their fathers, and I wanted that…I needed that. My home life wasn't ideal, and the relationship I had with my mother was lacking. I thought if he would just see me, see that the little odd bumps of extra skin at the end of my fingertips matched his, he couldn't reject me…after all, he made me. With hope in my heart, I thought there was no way that I would allow myself to be fatherless for the rest of my life.

After a great deal of continual searching for a new realm of information, a phone number populated…I dialed and waited in fear; no one answered, in fact, the dreaded automated "this number has been disconnected or is out of service" voice shattered my hopes. At that point I knew there might be no chance of me ever getting to see the man who contributed to my existence, I knew it was over.

I had accepted the label of 'fatherless' as a 'forever' brand in my life. As absurd as this sounds, that moment was everything to me… that was what God had ultimately been waiting for. He was waiting for me to need Someone who could not be given through a worldly realm, someone who could love on a level that I could not fathom.

Accepting the circumstances that life has thrown at you, accepting yourself as fatherless, whether (physical or spiritual), allows you to accept a new Father, it allows for you to be filled with Someone who can love you as you should have been and should be, loved.

Reflection

Can you recall a pivotal moment that reminded you of the absence of your father? The moment that you accepted fatherless.

_____

_____

_____

_____

_____

_____

Explain in detail what led you to this point. What led you to the pivotal moment?

_____

_____

_____

_____

_____

_____

If that moment is now, what led you to read this text? Is it a coincidence?

_____

_____

_____

_____

_____

_____

_____

_____

Chapter 5

RELINQUISH YOUR PAST

*I*F YOU WERE AROUND DURING the nineties, you were present when Lindsay Lohan rose to stardom in her debut of *Parent Trap* (and other Disney movies).

Lindsay had a double role in this movie where she played herself and her 'twin sister' who came from completely different lives because of a divorce.

Ironically, these twins knew nothing about each other until they became acquainted at the mall. They exposed their lives to one another, realizing they shared a common denominator, parents that were once together and then split. They decided to switch wardrobes and go home with the parents they had been alienated from. During this switch, Hallie and Annie spent time with their dreaded stepmother who hadn't the slightest clue how to become a cherished and loved mother. These stories of evil stepmothers/fathers are notorious and often leave a bad taste in your mouth for any other parental fill in[7].

If you're not aware of the truth, you may think this new proposal of accepting yourself as fatherless means being vulnerable or in a position to replace your father with someone who will do the same to

---

[7] Nancy Meyers, *The Parent Trap.* Featuring Lindsay Lohan. Produced by Charles Shyer, 1998

you or your family...leave you stranded. Or maybe you're unsure if your spirit even needs a father as you've been pedaling this bike with no assistance for far too long. You've got this under control you tell yourself, until you don't. You've aged and begun to realize that your legs don't work as well as they used to, and now you need a bit of company as you ride that bike...to ensure you don't ride over a rock and fall. By the same token, spiritually, don't let yourself get to that point, and don't grow older and unable to ride without assistance, accept the help now.

Although you may be hesitant to believe this, nothing about God exemplifies a stepparent situation. The Lord has always been your Father...He created you just as He created your father and your mother; in His image (Genesis 1:27, New International Version). Your biological parents were merely the 'temps' of parenting. With our circumstances, we will realize that nothing is a coincidence... that there is a divine intervention. Everything that has happened has led you to this moment....to Christ, to guide you forever more. God will never ever forsake you as your biological father may have; He will never leave you...I mean it...when the world leaves you empty... He will be there.

Most of us reviewing this material may have trust issues after dealing with an absentee father, we either cling to the physical relationships we have, or we don't let anyone too close to us as referenced above. It may be hard to wrap your head around this one, you may be even weary, but please give God a try. His plan is that of comfort and completion, something many of us haven't had in a while (Deuteronomy 31:6, New International Version).

In the New Testament book of Matthew, Jesus, literally God in the flesh, calls to us **"Come to me, all who labor and are heavy laden, and I will give you rest…. Take my yoke upon you, and learn from me, for I am gentle and lowly in heart, and you will find rest for your souls. For my yoke is easy and my burden is light."** (Matthew 11:28-30, English Standard Version).

Pre-existent (have always existed) God/ Jesus/the Holy Spirit may be viewed, as divine symbols of comfort and paternal instruction; they are instruments of paternal love. God says through Matthew, if the yoke of this world is too heavy, come to Him. When coming to Him, He will soothe every one of us. He says to take His yoke, accepting Him to come into our hearts via the Holy Spirit (a much lighter weight that He carries with you), and learn from the way of the Teacher, Jesus. Jesus the humble servant leader, can teach us the way to progress in this world in a manner that satisfies our longing while being an instrument to others. That lends us to an eternal life without pain, without suffering, replacing a life of bitterness and contempt with one of peace and forgiveness because God forgave our sins. When accepting Him as our Father, we no longer perish within the mental, emotional, or physical life, but begin to enjoy a life of eternal bliss.

If today you are eager for Something/Someone to fill the void that has been empty for too long, you must consider Jesus, you must be willing to allow Him to assume the position, and you must trust Him.

You must assume fatherless...to allow yourself to be filled with the Father, in order to correct all the wrongs in your life that not even you could have controlled.

Are you ready to join alongside the brother and sisterhood in Christ? To join hands with the Father, to be comforted and loved for the rest of your remaining physical life, and be forever more within the eternal? If so, it would behoove you to read the scriptures listed below. These will give you more theological application of what I've been saying through the God breathed Word. BibleGateway is a great online resource for free; I recommend the New King James Version (NKJV), New International Version (NIV) or the English Standard Version (ESV) for newer readers.

It's great to be informed before you decide. After reading these, feel free to review the below prayer of salvation, you can alter the feelings to your own liking, but it must include repentance, understanding the payment of your sins through Jesus' work on the Cross and his resurrection, and an acceptance of Jesus into your heart (otherwise known as baptism of the Holy Spirit). Jesus is the gateway to the Father, as no one comes to the Father except through Jesus Christ (John 14:6).

Reflection Scriptures

Galatians 4:4-5 (born to save) (English Standard Version)

1 Timothy 1:15-17 (born to save) (English Standard Version)

Matthew 27:11-65 (death) (English Standard Version)

Matthew 28: 1-20 (resurrection and great commission) (English Standard Version)

Salvation scriptures

Romans 3:23 (English Standard Version)

Romans 5:6-8 (English Standard Version)

Romans 10:1, 9-11 (English Standard Version)

An eternal Oath, a prayer for salvation

Dear Lord,

I am sorry for carrying the load of this hurt on my back by myself for so long, it has been tough, and I am starting to believe that there is something more beneficial out there for me in You.

It seems that Your plans have always been to comfort me in this chaotic game of chess called life, yet I have ignored Your attempts.

The pain was so gruesome that it masked my judgment and caused feelings inside me that I didn't even know I possessed, and I no longer want to handle it on my own. I no longer want to live without a Father.

It has been shown to me that You sent Yourself in human form as Jesus to die for my sins, which I am so grateful for. Then after dying, you rose again (Luke 24, English Standard Version) to live within us.

I want this, God; I ask that You forgive me for avoiding the situation, forgive me for my sins; please enter my life; please fill the void that is only meant to be filled by You. I am so sorry you had to pay for my sins, but I am also very grateful. I repent of my sins and accept your free gift of salvation.

Thank You for saving me.
Amen.

<u>Verses to hold Dear</u>

"Sing to God, sing in praise of His name, extol Him who rides on the clouds, rejoice before Him—His name is the Lord. A Father to the fatherless, a defender to the widows, is God in His holy dwelling".[8]

"If you declare with your mouth, 'Jesus is Lord,' and believe in your heart that God raised Him from the dead, you will be saved. (Romans 10:9, New International Version)

---

[8] Psalm 68:4-5, New King James Version

"Therefore, if anyone is in Christ, the new creation has come: The old has gone, the new is here!"
(2 Corinthians 5:17, New International Version)

"Jesus answered, 'I am the way and the Truth and the Life. No one comes to the Father except through me'." (John 14:6, New International Version)

"Doubtless you are our Father, though Abraham was ignorant of us, and Israel does not acknowledge us…you o Lord are our Father; Our Redeemer from Everlasting is Your name" (Isaiah 63:16-17, New King James Version)

"I have found David my servant;
with my sacred oil I have anointed him.
My hand will sustain him;
surely my arm will strengthen him.
The enemy will not get the better of him;
the wicked will not oppress him.
I will crush His foes before him
and strike down His adversaries.
My faithful love will be with him,
and through my name His horn will be exalted.
I will set His hand over the sea,
His right hand over the rivers.
He will call out to me, 'You are my Father,
my God, the Rock my Savior'."
(Psalm 89:20-26, New King James Version)

Transitional Note from Author

Up until this point, we have spoken about my experience, understanding what our own circumstances were and what aided in the title 'fatherless'. How this affected us, and how our perception of replacing our father may feel. We arrived at a point of acceptance of this label, and then we introduced the concept of being filled with the Father…. otherwise known as salvation.

If you chose to follow Jesus above, I highly recommend you link up with your nearest Bible (gospel-centric) believing church and discuss the topic of baptism. It is an outward attestation of the inward choice, and follows as an act of obedience…you were already baptized with the Holy Spirit if you asked Him into your life and prayed the above prayer. You are a new being in Christ, a saved being, but you need to be protected…like a fresh bald eagle baby coming into the world for the first time. Predators still attempt to grab that baby despite it being an eagle. Find a good church, and look towards the Lord.

As I mentioned in the introduction, Fatherful can be immediate, but it is also continual…consider the process again like an organism that needs to be fed to survive. In your walk you can grow distracted, and fall back into the trap of faulty thinking and of sin (thank the great predator, Satan for this) so you must put up boundaries or guard rails of thinking if you'd like to grow. I still make mistakes and I've been saved for fifteen years…it's easy to do. In the following sections I will briefly touch some afterthought categories, of what to look out for as you grow to be Fatherful, and how to immerse yourself in healthy practices that through the assistance of the triune God could lend to upward trajectory. I pray for a journey of ease and beauty in every corner of your route. Welcome to the family of Christ; we have the same Father, isn't that lovely? I love you, brother or sister.

Chapter 6
ACCEPTING SUFFERING P1.

$\mathcal{I}$'D LIKE TO FIRST PREFACE the idea of 'accepting suffering' not as a mechanism to perpetuate abuse or mistreatment of any kind; God calls you to peace (1 Corinthians 7:15, English Standard Version) and will talk to you specifically about your own situations/circumstances and will lead you in the decisions you must take. God loves His people and brings justice to those who treat His creation as anything less than His (Romans 12:19, English Standard Version).

Accepting Suffering? The title of this chapter alone could make you cringe, shut this book, and turn on your favorite Netflix season.

As daunting as it sounds, don't leave me now, the glory in the end will be worth reading this chapter.

I had just bought a beautifully blessed house, the thing had everything I ever wanted and more in a shell of walls and for a humble price compared to the housing market I had been used to (did I mention that I moved from California to Pennsylvania...that pretty much sums it up...no shade here).

The interior was even acceptable with its purple kitchen, yellow sunroom, purple bath tiles, purple rugs, and green showers and toilets. I could totally have lived in a house with a rainbow interior, after all, rainbow is my son's favorite color. He had no issues with the sunset mural in his bedroom, he even got upset when I began to tear it down. Whatever the case, I can vulnerably attest that I have 'Yuppie vision' as an interior decorator (if you have ever seen the famous duck hunting family show you know what I'm talking about)[9]. Although I am not one to care about material possessions, if I have the ability to choose, I would prefer a darker stained mantel in opposition to a walnut, and a new vanity/sink/faucet combination rather than putting a new top on an old outdated cabinet...yep.... yuppie I am. We all have preferences.

When closing on the house, it was frequented at least every day to work on minor cosmetic improvements. As I say 'minor cosmetic improvements', I am reminded of the groaning and moaning about the pain endured from the workload. The pain was accepted, however, because the pain had to be gone through to get the result. In the end, the floors looked great.

In relation to this illustration, at creation, God had every intention to make our way pure, to pave a path of ease everywhere we went, without suffering. God created us as a mirror representation of Himself, first Adam, from dust, and later, his wife, Eve, whom he created by causing Adam to fall into a deep sleep and removing a rib (the first operation!). Adam and Eve were placed within the Garden of Eden and given dominion over every living creature and seed-bearing plant on the earth. God then instructed them that they could eat from any tree within the garden except the tree that provided knowledge of good and evil. After that, He introduced wild animals for Adam to name and care for, with Eve as his helper. Serpents were included within the wild animals created, but one slithery, slimy serpent (Satan, the deceiver) desired more than he had access to. He desired to be more powerful and worshipped more than God. In wanting this, he found the perfect opportunity to manipulate. He saw Adam and Eve as an easy target, especially after knowing what God had told them. If he could just confuse

---

[9] Duck Dynasty, directed by Jonathan Haug, Hugh Peterson, David Hobbes, Hisham Abed, and Tara Delaney, The Robertson's. 2012-2017

them about the reality of what they heard, he would lead them to stumbling, and thus have an ounce of what he wanted. In his attempt, he tested Eve's memory by saying; "Did God really say, 'You must not eat from any tree in the garden'?" (Genesis 3:1, New International Version). He put a question into her head (and this is exactly why you need a hedge of protection against the enemy; Psalm 34:7). Unfortunately, Eve was deceived, along with Adam, as they both consumed the fruit of the tree (some say it was an apple, but we can't be sure what kind of fruit it was).

From that point on, sin and suffering entered the world; their eyes were opened as they suddenly realized that they were naked (they hadn't known until that point; Genesis 2:25, ESV). As you may do when someone accidently pops open the door that you forgot to lock while using the restroom, they immediately scurried to sew fig leaves together to cover themselves from one another and hid from God as he approached. Hurry, grab the TP! Cover yourself!

God knew their actions before even asking, and because of this deliberate attempt at skirting the instruction they were given, He disciplined them, as we were when we disobeyed in our youth.

The result was a curse on the serpent (Satan):

> *14 So the Lord God said to the serpent, "Because you have done this, cursed are you above all livestock and all wild animals! You will crawl on your belly and you will eat dust all the days of your life.*
> *15 And I will put enmity between you and the woman, and between your offspring and hers; He will crush your head, and you will strike His heel."* (Genesis 3:14-15; NIV).

Special Note: within this verse is our Salvation: He (Jesus) will crush Satan's head (he will defeat Satan by his work on the Cross), although Satan will try numerous times to defeat Him ('strike his heel').

A curse on women:

> *To the woman, he said, "I will make your pains in childbearing very severe; with painful labor, you will give birth to children. Your desire will be for your husband, and he will rule over you."* (Genesis 3:16; NIV)

And a curse on man (mankind):

> *[17] To Adam he said, "Because you listened to your wife and ate fruit from the tree about which I commanded you, 'You must not eat from it,' "Cursed is the ground because of you; through painful toil you will eat food from it all the days of your life.*
> *[18] It will produce thorns and thistles for you, and you will eat the plants of the field.*
> *[19] By the sweat of your brow you will eat your food until you return to the ground, since from it you were taken; for dust you are and to dust you will return."* (Genesis 3:17-19; NIV)

Since they are the parents of ALL mankind, we, through no fault of our own, reap the consequences of that fall. Suffering is a normal part of our lives.

If you review the Old Testament of the Bible, you will realize the characters of the OT dealt with the consequences of Adam and Eve's sin through many sacrifices, pain, and loss...the Payment (Jesus) for sin was yet to come.

The suffering referenced in Genesis is imminent whether you're saved, whether you've accepted Fatherful, or not; it happens to everyone in various forms. Because of the fall, mankind must endure suffering, and it truly is awful.

There is, however, good news!! If you have a Bible, or Bible app handy and you look to the first 4 books of the New Testament (what we call the gospels, Matthew/Mark/Luke/John), you will see that God loved us ALL so much that regardless of what happened with Adam and Eve, He sent His only Son to withstand heinous punishment on the Cross so that you don't have to eternally suffer for the consequences of sin. You have a way to avoid the punishment that happens to everyone who is disciplined for their wrong choices, a chance to inherit the eternal life of glory in Heaven and be without the suffering of eternal death (John 3:16, English Standard Version).

Whatever circumstance you have gone through that has robbed you of a parental role (or anything for that matter), has indeed been traumatizing...there's no doubt about that. There is nothing fair about suffering, we are not happy about that. Lamentation is completely normal and necessary; life will not be easy without your biological father and as anticipated it's totally normal to expect grief. God says blessed are those who mourn because they will be comforted.

If life were perfect, we would have absolutely no room for God, we would have absolutely no room for others. Remember that this is not the life that He originally had in store for us.

This suffering, our suffering has a purpose even if it is gruesome to accept, much like the flooring installation mentioned earlier. There is a glorious ending that will be seen full circle when we're done installing the flooring, after the aches and pains. The purpose can only be fulfilled with the appropriate tools and adequate equipment, spiritually it's when we fill ourselves with the Father.

Someone asked me, "If you never were disappointed would you think that you would ever have a use for God?" It's true, man will always disappoint us, but we have an alternative form of support that replaces the disappointment from the world.

The Bible says, **"His grace is sufficient for us, His power is made perfect in weakness"** (2 Corinthians 12:9, English Standard Version) ...weakness a societal characteristic that we discard is shown beautiful in the kingdom.

Man will continue to disappoint us, it's the sad truth, but we live in a world of options, yet trusting Him is a tested and true decision. Accepting God and focusing on Him allows for a mitigation of disappointment.

If you ask(ed) God into your life and set the role as not only your Father but your personal savior[10], making a commitment to walk with Him wherever He goes then you can be confident that your name is in the Book of Life preparing you for eternal glory.

The last book of the Bible, the book of Revelation, talks about the end days, those who are not saved residing on Earth during the judgments, the apocalypse, as opposed to the life believers will look forward to in Heaven; a life of eternal glory. Revelation 21:

> "**[3] And I heard a loud voice from the throne saying, "Look! God's dwelling place is now among the people, and He will dwell with them. They will be His people, and God Himself will be with them and be their God. [4] 'He will wipe every tear from their eyes. There will be no more death'[c] or mourning or crying or pain, for the old order of things has passed away."**
>
> **[5] He who was seated on the throne said, "I am making everything new!" Then He said, "Write this down, for these words are trustworthy and true."**
>
> **[6] He said to me: "It is done. I am the Alpha and the Omega, the Beginning and the End. To the thirsty, I will give water without cost from the spring of the water of life.[7] Those who are victorious will inherit all this, and I will be their**

God and <u>they will be my children</u>. (Revelation 21:3, New International Version)

First and foremost, let's invite over the guy who always tells us that 'Nothing in this life is ever free', fake news. God said to the thirsty…I will give water…without cost. That's you and me, friend. I'll speak for us; you don't even have to mutter it yourself just yet… we are hungry (like 4 plates at the Chinese buffet hungry) and we are hungry for a Father. We have suffered our whole lives (or for a period) because of the absence of our father, this hunger has bled into every not-so-right area of our lives and festered.

But it doesn't have to be like this anymore[11], there is someone who can give us exactly what we need, and if you have agreed upon that at this point you know I'm talking about THE FATHER. He says those who have triumphed and understood that they are thirsty/ hungry will inherit the goodness of NO-SUFFERING[12]. They say caps-locks are to be avoided when writing but it's completely necessary here. He says that because we have accepted Him into our lives and admitted, we are so famished without Him, once we get to heaven, once He returns, He will wipe every single tear that we have cried[13]. Remember that this decision has to happen for eternal glory, those who do not make the decision of accepting Him as the Father will not see such a gift. It's a sad truth that we must accept, however in the end as coming to salvation…death won't exist, mourning or crying about our past pain will be no longer…because we will be in His presence[14].

Those verses make my once-Fatherless heart so happy. No longer will I suffer when I get to Heaven, no longer will I have trials or tribulations, I won't even remember what suffering is and neither will you. Accepting suffering in this life will be worth the glory in

---

[11] See above page on salvation

[12] Matthew 25:34, English Standard Version

[13] 1 Samuel 20:41, English Standard Version

[14] Revelations 21:4, English Standard Version

the next, and much more appealing than my yuppie renovations and the back-breaking labor that goes with it.

Reflection

Can you think of an example of a time when suffering was worth the end result? How did you feel afterward? Document below.

_____

_____

_____

_____

_____

_____

_____

Besides our fathers, have you been disappointed in man?

_____

_____

_____

_____

_____

_____

Did you know before this text that God had a plan for us of a pleasant life without suffering? Knowing this, and remembering the fallible actions of man, does this help with your own idea of grace for others?

_____

_____

_____

_____

_____

_____

Can you foresee anything positive becoming of your situation as 'fatherless'? Maybe for the next generation of individuals? List a few illustrations of how below.

_____

_____

_____

_____

_____

_____

_____

_____

Chapter 7
ACCEPTING SUFFERING P2.

My ETERNAL FATHER AND I met in Gatlinburg (thanks to my pastor for helping), Tennessee, while I was face down on the floor of a loft in a cabin that my youth group had rented. A friend had led me to the church and I had heard of God but had no recollection that it demanded an actual acceptance, a relationship, a filling of the Holy Spirit. In my naivety, I believed if you believed in God, and were a 'good person' you were good to go! Then I heard **"There is none that doeth good, no not one"** (Romans 3:10-12, King James Version), and at that point, it hit me, I wasn't really all that good.

My mother had sent me to a very small church every Sunday by myself from around eight years of age to thirteen…she was going through her own trials. She had lost her mother and father around the birth of her first child and had no support system and no sense of receiving affection from anyone either. She was seeking love, as well, and enjoyed her time alone.

I never liked to go by myself, because, what eight-year-old likes to go to a church with no young people? It was rough, but they had free van pickup (we never had a car) and it kind of made me forget about my home situation for a bit. I knew of the Lord but didn't know that accepting Him as my savior was a part of it…and my life reflected that. I stayed to myself, my confidence in my appearance and abilities was lacking, and I became wayward, drinking alcohol and hanging with the wrong crowd by age 16. Though I had attended church at a young age, I had denied going when asked and started to hang out with new friends who had invited me into their lives; these friends were into drugs and alcohol, but I always had a firm foundation of inner morality, or so I thought.

My brother had joined the military and was stationed overseas for most of my youth, and my sister was much older and into her own thing. In addition, my mother was nearing the end of her child-rearing stages (I was the last), so she began to enjoy her life more liberally, and, as a result, I took advantage of being left alone.

I didn't go wild, but when I began to realize what was happening at home, I dived into alcohol myself and enjoyed the ride (self-induced suffering). I had rebelled against my mother, and at times I harbored hatred for her up until I allowed God to fill the role that lacked in my life. From sixteen to twenty, I still tried earthly ways to make myself feel worthy of love through other men, premarital relations, pictures, anything… they all ended in suffering.

In retrospect nothing was my mother's fault (and I'm sure of the same in your life even if we'd like to chalk it up that way), it wasn't even my father's…it was the serpent's, but the suffering was there and it has molded and assisted me into who I am today. As does the same for you. Your sorrow leads to repentance (2 Corinthians 7:9, English Standard Version paraphrased).

I am nothing like who I was when I was twenty, but those lessons led me to Christ, that suffering enabled a need for something bigger…to accept Christ, to share with you all. Jesus Christ, the Father of comfort gives us this comfort within our suffering so that we likewise can comfort those who are in trouble (2 Corinthians 1:3-4, English Standard Version paraphrased).

Of those who have a relationship with the triune God/Jesus/Holy Spirit, we count our suffering as joy, because we agree in our common denominator of imperfection. James mentioned that our longsuffering has a purpose, to produce fruit in us that is impossible by ourselves (James 1:2-4, English Standard Version), to ultimately bring others to Christ.

When invited, I accepted. God led me to Gatlinburg to know Him and accept Him because He knew what I had experienced because He loved me more than those who hurt me could. In the same way, you may have dealt with similar thoughts. This is what we call a testimony, and it has a purpose for other generations...a purpose you will later see.

If you feel your soul strings resonating with that story or something else has popped up into your mind after reading this, I'm sure it's intentional. God is the ultimate caregiver; He can deliver us from any bit of suffering because He is much stronger than the one who lives to stir up strife.... the 'god' of this world.

Reflection

Has anyone in your life invited you to go to church? What about mentioning God? What sort of experiences do you recall dealing with religion or spirituality? List them below

_____

_____

_____

_____

_____

_____

_____

Do you find it a coincidence that you are invited to the Lord today? Is there a possibility that the interactions had a correlation to reviewing this material?

_____

_____

_____

_____

_____

_____

_____

What has been your experience with the word 'long suffering'? If you've heard this word used in church, did you discover the purpose behind it?

_____

_____

_____

_____

_____

_____

_____

_____

Knowing now what you didn't know then, how will this information shape your experiences from this point forward?

_____

_____

_____

_____

_____

_____

_____

_____

Chapter 8

THE ENEMY'S INTENTIONS

$\mathcal{W}$E LEFT OFF ON THE last chapter with a cliffhanger, which was intentional. You may say to yourself, "I thought the God of this world was God"? Let's carry on into deeper discovery of what I said.

Some people turn their backs on God because they say, 'why would a loving God hurt others?'. 'Why would He allow this or that calamity to happen?' 'Why would He take away my father to make me in pain this whole time?' It has affected so much of my life…it has destroyed me. This thought seems correct, but it is far from it. The god of pain, the god of this world is Satan, and it was not God's intention to allow for suffering to happen. It was not His intention to create evil, evil happened through pride.

In the first chapter of Genesis God created this world 'GOOD'… not evil…and then by chapter three of Genesis, the evil happens. As referenced in Ezekiel 28:12-17 (NIV), many scholars believe that this is a direct reference to what happened to the opposer (Satan) and the introduction of evil into our world. It says:

"You were the seal of perfection,

full of wisdom and perfect in beauty
(indicating that Satan had once been
an angel, a created being).

**You were in Eden the garden of God
and anointed as a guardian cherub**

(Having some sort of authority)
for so I ordained you...

You were blameless (he was made blameless
in the form of an angel) **and then you were
found wicked** (Genesis account of him taking
the form of a serpent and tricking Adam and
Eve to eat from the Tree of Knowledge).

**Because of this wickedness, you were filled
with violence and you as an angel sinned.**

**So, I drove you from the superiority of
my pure angels and expelled you**

**O guardian cherub from amongst your
blessings to the earth. You allowed your heart**

(because of your position) **to grow
prideful and become fixated**

**on your beauty and it corrupted your
wisdom and allowed you to fall."**

Later in Corinthians, he is later
identified as the 'God of this world'.

**"Satan, who is the god of this world, has
blinded the minds of those who don't
believe. They are unable to see the glorious
light of the Good News. They don't
understand this message about the glory of
Christ, who is the exact likeness of God."**
(2 Corinthians 4:4, New International Version)

I've written an entire chapter about this enemy of ours to show you the contrast between good and evil, and to inform you that he was created to be available, as are all angels, to carry out God's wishes, but grew prideful in his abilities and was cast down to the earth to reign. If he had not been manipulative in his attempts to thwart righteousness, suffering would not be prevalent today. Recalling, God had intended to share His creation with us, a place that had no division, a place without suffering, no evil, no wars, and a place of peace. (Genesis account of creation, ESV)

God mentioned to Adam and Eve after placing them in the Garden of Eden that they could eat from any tree, but not the tree of Knowledge of Good and Evil. They were instructed, that they would die if they ate from that tree. The serpent used the pride that he had built up in himself to manipulate the word of God and attack the very weakness of Eve. He allowed for confusion; he crafted the words in such a manner that Eve would question what the true words were that God said. He wanted dominion over her, over the earth… and that's what he received. To this day he causes the people of our earth pain, and his angel comrades who were tainted with him, aid in this action to be performed.[15]

He knows that you, especially if you have accepted the Lord as your Father, are now capable of being on fire for Christ. On fire for making the kingdom move and gain more followers for Jesus. When you take from Satan, he doesn't like that, or even the threat of it. So, you must guard your heart and your life because, like Eve, he will seek to devour you…like a roaring lion (1 Peter 5:8, English Standard Version paraphrased). You might be saying "what in the world did I sign up for??!" my response "chilllllllll" (Millennial lingo here). Despite this overarching theme of power, our Redeemer has more strength than any beast on the earth, and even the demons and Satan listen to Him. When you invited Him in, you received a piece of Him (the Holy Spirit) inside of you.

---

[15] Revelations 12:4, English Standard Version

Again, remember that God wanted you to have an earthly father, a perfect nuclear family. He wanted you to be adored, treasured, uplifted as a child of God...but, through sin, that all changed. If you need someone to blame for your fatherless circumstances, it is not you, it's not your father even, and it surely is not God (although he is tough enough to take the blame). God never wanted this for you. It was and still is the serpent...the one who prowls this earth like a lion seeking who he will devour; the one who comes only to steal and destroy (John 10:10); he is the one to blame.

Let's commit to avoid the traps set aside for us to fall into, because satan will be setting them through 'easier ways out', through pride, through lies, even though worldly success and fortune. Fatherless was a trap, but we're not going to let it catch us any further. Fatherless has not destroyed you, it has instead equipped you with the skillset to win the race.

<u>Reflections</u>

Have you ever participated in a sport or competition where you had a very strong opponent? What did you do to remain focused? To avoid overanalyzing the position and psyching yourself out? Write your methods below.

_____

_____

_____

_____

_____

_____

Chapter 9

FATHERFUL REQUIRES
ABSOLUTE FAITH

*H*AVE YOU EVER PLAYED A subconscious game with those close to you? Knowing what's going on but not saying a thing to one another? Kind of like the game of Chameleon.[16] My former roommate and I used to unknowingly play a game of who's going to take the trash out today. Though there may have been a bit of confusion as to whose role it was to take out the trash, an expectation of the trash being on the curb by Thursday was solidified (or we won't have enough room for the next week's trash accumulation). This minuscule act of having faith in each other helped keep things together; it allowed for an act to be performed so the next week's plans went smoothly.

In the book of Matthew, Chapter 9[17], the Apostle Matthew wrote about the many healings and activities that had happened throughout Jesus's day. In particular, while Jesus was speaking to John's disciples, someone approached Him to heal their daughter who had just passed away. In the act of Him turning towards the man's kin to revive her, another lady who had been bleeding nonstop for twelve years thought to herself..." If I just put my hand on this man's cloak, His healing abilities will consume me and make

---

[16] Chameleon, Silver Wish Games, 2005
[17] English Standard Version

me well". Jesus immediately turned from what He was already in pursuit of healing, and acknowledged the woman saying "Take heart, daughter; your faith has healed you" (Matthew 9:14-22, NIV).

Jesus was planning to heal another who was dead…let's repeat that…He was seconds away from healing the dead, when He stopped everything, He was doing and noticed the faith of someone else and healed her first. This story is one of my favorites in the Bible. Not only was Jesus on a healing spree making miraculous events happen, but He paused in the act of healing and healed someone else because she knew in her heart that if her fingertips only touched His linen garment, she would be better. I mean, to be honest, there were times when I really didn't have faith in my roommate to take out the garbage, so I looked out the window to make sure it was on the curb when I woke up on Thursday morning. In comparison to my lack of faith in my roommate, the faith in the instance of the woman is admirable.

This shows us that if we just have an inkling of faith, in Him, in His being our Father, He can run with it. When we ask God to mend our wounds, we need to let go of the reins and have absolute faith in Him to heal us completely. It may take a little while to have the faith mentioned in these Biblical instances, but when we do, instead of grabbing His hem we instead grab Him. Grab Him just like our children/nieces/nephews took our hands as we walked across the street. We need to grab His hand and permit Him to be our security and safehold, just like the youngsters do with their fathers; after all He is our Father now.

Fatherful Actions

Can you think of instances in your life that you have avoiding attaching faith to? Write them below:

_____

_____

_____

_____

_____

_____

_____

In which ways can you relinquish control over those issues and let God deliver?

_____

_____

_____

_____

_____

_____

_____

_____

_____

REE DEEMD

Open your Bible to the concordance in the back, look up the word 'faith', and review a few scriptures correlating with the word. Write your favorite below and meditate on their meaning to your new life.

_____

_____

_____

_____

_____

_____

_____

_____

In what ways have you already given God faith? In which ways have you given yourself faith?

_____

_____

_____

_____

_____

_____

_____

_____

_____

Chapter 10

BEING FATHERFUL – READING HIS WORD

I'LL START THIS OUT WITH this simple point, Christianity is a relationship, not a works-based religion. Nothing you can do will make you a better person, or more worthy in God's eyes. In the same manner, nothing you do wrong will make you less worthy. The Pharisees and Sadducees didn't understand this, they had grown accustomed to the law of Moses, the commandments, the Torah, the Law. They had been devout worshippers of God and His commandments, and when Jesus arrived, they couldn't fathom any other way…they saw it all as blasphemy. Jesus came so that we were freed from the law (Romans 6:14[18]) and although the Law is still useful, it is salvation through faith that sets you free (Romans 3:19-27-30[19]).

The Holy Spirit, imparted to us at salvation, gives us a great hunger and thirst for righteousness (Matthew 5:6[20]), and in this hunger, we find ourselves with a desire to be obedient. It's similar to what you would expect a nuclear family to have for the leaders of the household.

---

[18] English Standard Version
[19] Ibid.
[20] Ibid.

Who then is an obedient child of God? **"The greatest commandment of all is to love the Lord your God with all your heart, soul, and mind...second to this is love thy neighbor as oneself"** (Matthew 22:37[21]). This proves to be in direct opposition to what our world tells us to do. "Love yourself", "do you", "YOLO", "if it doesn't hurt others and you're happy it's ok", "follow your heart", or a favorite, "you can do whatever you want to do". These thoughts, common today, are contrary to 'love your God above everyone'[22], as well as 'loving others as yourself'[23], still, it should be done.

Loving the Lord our God; how can we do that? As Jesus walked on earth and taught His disciples how to learn and follow their Teacher, He said some very important things – "learn from me...for I am gentle and lowly in heart" (Matthew 11:28-30, NIV). A second exhortation is to be like Christ as much as possible. We cannot be like Him if we don't spend the time and effort in researching who He was. Utilize His word, which is literally alive to direct your path. It says that the word is "a lamp unto your feet, and a light unto your path" (Psalm 119:105, NIV), practice by operating the flashlight.

The text is set up as such, the Old Testament, the historical account of Jewish lineage and testimony of happenings, and the New Testament, where Jesus came and lived for thirty -three years, to then die for our sins and rise again on the third day, and fill each and every one of your hearts alongside with invitation. Both texts are applicable.

Someone once told me to start in Romans, which I did, using the King James Version; go ahead and do that if you're feeling up to the challenge. I recommend using the New King James Version, (NKJV), the New International Version (NIV) or the English Standard Version (ESV), and, if you can find one with a commentary,

---

[21] Ibid.
[22] Matthew 22:35-40, ESV
[23] Matthew 22:37-39, ESV

that will be even more helpful. You will notice my use of different translations, to, hopefully, provide a clear understanding of the text.

Some pastors and scholars are very specific to their translation, claiming that anything other than the original King James version waters down the original intention of the text. Get with your local pastor to discuss options or shoot me an email and I will be happy to assist you. The scriptures are not set up in chronological order, or timeline of events…it can get a little confusing, but be brave, the Holy Spirit will assist in your interpretation and application. It is no hyperbole that the word is alive, and it will amaze you. My best advice when reading through the Bible is to have a pen and a journal handy and stop when something jolts your senses or calls to you to write it down. I have several journals highlighting topics that I have categorized by thought and relevant scriptures. BTW – it is not sacrilegious to make notes or highlight important verses in the Bible. The Lord will shape you through His word, and you will be amazed at your ability to recall verses (with the assistance of the Holy Spirit, I've done it quite a few times throughout this text…thanks be to God), when you need them.

"For the word of God is quick, and powerful, and sharper than any two-edged sword, piercing even to the dividing asunder of soul and spirit, and of the joints and marrow, and is a discerner of the thoughts and intents of the heart" (Hebrews 4:12, NIV)

How exciting is it to know information and share it with others? Plan to keep consistency, find a quiet time to study daily, asking God to lead you in memory in understanding, in application, and in relationship with Him. Use the word to know Him, and to learn from Him and he will **"make your pathways straight"** (Proverbs 3:6, NIV).

Reflection

Do you own a Bible? What is the version you currently own? Flip a few pages; can you comprehend what it's saying to you (some are written in Olde English, which is very difficult to understand)?

_____

_____

_____

_____

_____

_____

What part of your day could you take advantage of in order to acquaint yourself with Jesus?

_____

_____

_____

_____

_____

_____

_____

Often, I get butterflies when studying new subjects, do you feel the same about your newest subject?

_____

_____

_____

_____

_____

_____

Make a plan below to be consistent with your devotion, I've heard it said that it takes a number of repetitions to make a habit…write down your plan…tear out this portion and post it somewhere for accountability purposes.

_____

_____

_____

_____

_____

_____

_____

_____

Chapter 11

BEING FATHERFUL – FINDING
A CHURCH FAMILY

I THINK THE MOST OUTRAGEOUS LIE we can tell ourselves or anyone else is that we don't need a church family. The truth is that each Christian is part of the body of Christ and that we each have a contribution to not only the much larger church (Christians amongst the world) but to those within our walls, and those outside of it…as a group.

This will be a large chunk of scripture, but I find it pertinent to share:

"One Body with Many Members"

¹² **For just as the body is one and has many members, and all the members of the body, though many, are one body, so it is with Christ.** ¹³ **For in one Spirit we were all baptized into one body—Jews or Greeks, slaves or free—and all were made to drink of one Spirit.**

¹⁴ **For the body does not consist of one member but of many.** ¹⁵ **If the foot should say, "Because I am not a hand, I do not belong to the**

body," that would not make it any less a part of the body. [16] And if the ear should say, "Because I am not an eye, I do not belong to the body," that would not make it any less a part of the body. [17] If the whole body were an eye, where would be the sense of hearing? If the whole body were an ear, where would be the sense of smell? [18] But as it is, God arranged the members in the body, each one of them, as He chose. [19] If all were a single member, where would the body be? [20] As it is, there are many parts, yet one body.

[21] The eye cannot say to the hand, "I have no need of you," nor again the head to the feet, "I have no need of you." [22] On the contrary, the parts of the body that seem to be weaker are indispensable, [23] and on those parts of the body that we think less honorable we bestow the greater honor, and our unpresentable parts are treated with greater modesty, [24] which our more presentable parts do not require. But God has so composed the body, giving greater honor to the part that lacked it, [25] that there may be no division in the body, but that the members may have the same care for one another. [26] If one member suffers, all suffer together; if one member is honored, all rejoice together.

[27] Now you are the body of Christ and individually members of it." (1 Corinthians 12:12-27, NIV)

'Periodt', Back to millennial talk here.

We all need each other to thrive to our fullest potential. The church's main purpose is to go and make disciples and send them to the end of the earth to share the gospel (Matthew 28:19-20[24]). They have a purpose with you in all your newness, to mentor and grow you in all your student desires so that you can do the same for others. I know it's daunting to join a congregation; you may think all eyes are on you…and they might be, but it's a warming acceptance of you, not a judgmental evaluation. The church is a hospital for the spiritually sick, not a trophy case for the upright. If they're living in the Spirit, they will be glad you're coming, and as you've accepted Christ; you will quickly find that your soul delights in going…so much so, that when you miss a service, you will feel it all week.

Do your research; not all facilities or congregations are the same; look up the doctrinal statement of the church you are interested in attending. It's usually on their website, loud and clear. Research what it says, things you don't know, and see if it aligns with the Bible and the gospel. There are churches out there that profess Jesus in the wrong light, the Spirit will let you know… avoid these and pray for them. Your church experience will usually include meeting with one another in the sanctuary, music, a sermon, and then an exit. There are often Bible studies in many churches before or after the main service, along with mid-week services…immerse yourself as much as you feel fit. You will retain quite a bit from these teachings. When you find a church that the Holy Spirit in you agrees with, find a few individuals to healthily cling to; they will gratefully mentor you along the way. Accountability partners are cherished members of any sisterhood in Christ and allow for true transparency that advances maturity. We all need someone who will remind us of the inside lines.

---

[24] English Standard Version

<u>Reflection</u>

Has anyone invited you to any church lately? Have you heard of any recently? How can you discover more information about the church?

Who is with you to guide you when things are wrong or right?

How can you rely on Him to guide your paths during this new stage of your life?

_____

_____

_____

_____

_____

_____

_____

What should a church's doctrine emulate?

_____

_____

_____

_____

_____

_____

_____

_____

Chapter 12

BEING FATHERFUL –
RELATIONSHIP WORK

*M*OST MARRIAGES IN THIS CURRENT age fail; why is that? For numerous reasons evidently, but one of them is that both partners are not on the same page of effort. The days of 80%/20% are no more (even if this is not an ideal standard) it's more like 95%/5%. In similarity to the lack of efforts, our relationship toward God can become stale when we slack in our efforts…in Christianity, we call this being 'lukewarm', neither hot nor cold…non effective.[25] No one likes a lukewarm bath…it doesn't make you feel warm enough when you're cold, yet it wouldn't be cool enough to enjoy on a hot day. In both efforts one would experience a truly disappointing outcome. In the same way, we want to ensure that we do not give ourselves as lukewarm Christians to our Redeemer the one with the likeness of a God, but also the warmth of a friend. We must commit to an effort to put God first. I said that correctly, He comes first, ahead of your marriage, yourself, your kids, your finances, your education your success…Him first. When we do this, all other things will be added to us (Matthew 6:31-33, English Standard Version).

I fail time and time again. I'm a mother of three under six, a divorcee, a full-time master's student, writing this book, while

---

[25] Revelation 3:15-18, ESV

enrolled in clinical pastoral education and a military chaplain candidate. Where does time for God come in? Here's the secret, you have to make time, because all other things even if they revolve around the idea of God, are not God. There's only one God, one Trinity (God/Jesus/Holy Spirit). Anything else that we hold in the place of God can become an idol...it can become legalism. Spend time in prayer daily: talking, writing, praying, thanking...this is your interaction, your communication. He needs to hear your soul, to see you're committed to showing it with your efforts. Most people do this in the morning before everyone else wakes, Jesus Himself retreated in silence from the crowds to spend time with the Father. He is supposed to be our illustration, and we should do the same.

In the movie 'The War Room', an elderly lady goes into her closet and pins her prayers on the walls, spending that time in retreat and meditation with God[26]. Similarly, the scripture states that when we pray, we should go into a room, shut the door, and pray to our Father in secret and our Father in secret will reward us (Matthew 6:6[27]). Our prayers aren't supposed to be big and mighty and expectant of a crowd (Matthew 6:5[28]), but intentional relationship building and of solitude. There is also no such thing as a bad prayer, and don't ever let someone tell you otherwise. Sometimes I get so tired and lose track of my words, then I am comforted by His word that states that He knows what we'll say before we say it and He will be there for us even when we make a mistake (Matthew 6:5-13[29]).

---

[26] War Room, Directed be Alex Kendrick, and written by Stephen Kendrick. Provident Films, Affirm Films, and TriStar Pictures, 2015.
[27] English Standard Version
[28] Ibid.
[29] Ibid.

Reflections

How can you be more intentional about your prayer life?

_____

_____

_____

_____

_____

_____

_____

_____

Were you aware that praying for acknowledgement from a crowd was in contrast to what scripture says?

_____

_____

_____

_____

_____

_____

_____

_____

_____

Do you have a quiet place where you can retreat? If not how can you construct one?

_____

_____

_____

_____

Are you excited to finally speak to your Father?

_____

_____

_____

_____

Even a simple prayer is still a prayer.

Try these:

Thank you, God for _____;
Lord, will you please help me with _____;
Lord, be with the people I just passed on the side of the road;
Lord, give me peace today as I endure impatient people;
Lord, please protect my children;
Lord, help me to honor you in my daily life;

These are just examples, anything can become of your prayers…let them be genuine, intimate, and just between you and Him…led by the Holy Spirit, from the depths of your heart.

Chapter 13

BEING FATHERFUL – SEEKING COUNSEL

$\mathcal{E}$ARLIER WITHIN THE TEXT IT was introduced that counseling is no longer as stigmatized as it was twenty years ago. In 2002 a whopping 27.2 million Americans opted in for mental health treatment or counseling, whereas in 2020 that number has nearly doubled.[30]

Part of realizing you are fatherless is also realizing that it affected you in some way. When God says that we're all part of the body, He means that in unison we work together perfectly. Without one of our members, we may not be as effective. Sans Biblical counseling, the restoration may take longer. I learned this the hard way and I'm begging you don't wait for that.

Employed as a hospice chaplain, I had a burning desire to give others what I wasn't given through the human form…love, acceptance, and comfort. This sort of thing happens naturally for us who have been wronged in some way, we somehow subconsciously think we can erase our pain by helping others with theirs first. The opposite is true, we need to work on ourselves and work on loving ourselves before we can love someone else.

---

[30] https://www.statista.com/statistics/794027/mental-health-treatment-counseling-past-year-us-adults/

Sort of thrown to the fishes, within twenty-four hours one of my first patients was nearing death…I sat alongside the family as they spoke to someone on their way out of life. I held their hands, hugged them, and delivered comfort to the best of my ability. That night I returned home with the same desire to distribute warmth to those in my community. I went to my elderly neighbor's house to check on their well-being and then back to my family. Within twenty-four hours I began to feel sick, and my infant daughter exhibited the same signs. Concerned for her well-being, we took her to the ER at our small local hospital due to low oxygen levels; she was taken by ambulance to a larger hospital, where she was diagnosed with COVID and severe dehydration. Later I received a text from the neighbor I'd visited, asking if we had COVID; the neighbors who were struggling with heart issues now had COVID. My heart sank, this was all my fault, I thought. (Update: thank God, they're fine now!). I knew at that moment I needed to seek counsel, not only to deal with what had happened, but because I had been assisting others in comfort during their dying moments, because the world around me didn't always see things the way I did. A heavy burden to be carried, it was essential that I be as healthy as possible.

I believed I had been dealing with the pain of my youth very well; I grew up strong and disciplined and swept it under the rug so no visitors would see it. Not having a father taught me how to be an alpha woman in society when I needed to be, defend others, and stand up when prompted. What I soon found out within a session or two is that I never let my 'inner child' feel. My therapist mentioned that when we are exposed to situations as children that cause us to fast forward our maturity, we run over our inner child and those feelings get muted. Like a tightrope that has never been walked on… the tension is tight, waiting for attention, waiting to feel. Thank the Lord for Godly counsel, because it turns out through my counselors' activities it was essential to more than just being a hospice chaplain.

Consider your experience in counseling as unpacking a deceased relative's luggage that has been sitting in your attic for quite some time. The suitcase is dusty, but it has valuables in it that need to be revisited; they need to be revisited because they teach you about yourself, through the memories contained within. Most importantly that suitcase needs to be unloaded, so you can travel again with others. Use this time with a helper as an opportunity to become versed in invigoration, to rebuild a house that may have had an uneven foundation, and to revisit self-esteem and confidence.

When choosing a 'helper' there are some things you should keep in mind, since we are all fallible creatures that demand infallible support. There are different avenues to request this help. Lay counselors in the church often have taken counseling courses but may not have the same credentials as a therapist or psychologist. Their approaches to healing differ as well, some use talk, and others use psychotherapy, and perhaps even medication. It's perfectly okay to choose a lay counselor or a Christian counselor…Know your objective - growth beyond yourself. Listen to the professional's advice, Counselors have an ethical standard that they need to abide by and are told to refer when necessary. If you hear this, don't take it as an insult, but consider it an expert giving you knowledge that you may or may not be versed in. Likewise, not all helpers are good at helping in this capacity; if you ever feel that what you're being told does not conform to the Bible, you should take careful consideration, maybe with the help of a Biblical mentor to trust but verify.

If you are worried about cost, usually pastors will do it for free because they believe that this is part of their calling. In addition, most modern-day health insurance plans can cover your corporate counseling visits, but if you would like to keep your sessions private, some assistants will work out an agreement based on their pricing structure and what you can afford. We must remember as well that we have aid and direct access to the Holy Spirit, Jesus and our Father who are capable of miracles. Open your Fatherful toolbox, and utilize prayer here, you can never do too much praying.

In all your efforts, be sure to be as transparent as possible…this allows for near-complete healing (complete healing comes from the

Father; remember, people are just conduits). You can't exactly get the assistance that you need for all your obstacles if you have one hidden under a rug. Confidentiality Is huge within the counseling community; most operate from a 'won't share confidential material unless harm to self or harm to others' or 'subpoenaed'. Military chaplains are a special category, however, and have one hundred percent confidentiality where they couldn't share an ounce of information with anyone if they wanted to. Do take the homework that they give you seriously, I know it seems silly, but what's more embarrassing than being in the same spot you're in ten years from now? Upward momentum is worth the illustrations.

Lastly, try not to get overwhelmed with choices, there are prevalent resources available to narrow down your search online, such as 'Faithful Counseling', 'Better Help', or 'Christian Counseling Directory'. Research, find one, and then commit to the big-brother/big-sister dichotomy; your future self will be grateful because of it. Feel free to journal your thoughts and experience as you step through this process, it will blow your mind how far you've come.

Reflections

What are some common misconceptions/stigmas that you've heard associated with seeking counsel?

_____

_____

_____

_____

_____

_____

Do you believe with the information you've received about being a part of a body of believers, that this has any logical backing? If so, how has society influenced that belief? If not, how?

_____

_____

_____

_____

_____

_____

_____

_____

How do you think the world would look if more people sought counseling? Do you think our interactions would improve?

_____

_____

_____

_____

_____

_____

_____

_____

If you were the first person in your family to seek counsel, do you think that would be an influential moment for them?

_____

_____

_____

_____

_____

_____

_____

_____

How can you commit to counseling?

_____

_____

_____

_____

_____

_____

_____

_____

Chapter 14
BEING FATHERFUL -
SPIRITUAL GIFTS

Discovering your Spiritual Gift(s) and using them

[10] God has given each of you a gift from His great variety of spiritual gifts. Use them well to serve one another. [11] Do you have the gift of speaking? Then speak as though God Himself were speaking through you. Do you have the gift of helping others? Do it with all the strength and energy that God supplies. Then everything you do will bring glory to God through Jesus Christ. All glory and power to Him forever and ever! Amen. [31]

THE LORD STATES THAT OUR gifts are for the purpose of bringing glory to God and bringing others to Him[32].

You may have heard of the Apostle Paul, who wrote many of the books of the New Testament…but he wasn't always the Apostle Paul. He was once a mean and evil man who persecuted Christians with

---

[31] 1 Peter 4:10-11, New Living Translation
[32] Ibid.

extreme prejudice. If you have the time, I recommend reviewing his conversion experience in Acts 9. Despite being a horrible person initially, following his salvation, he displayed a wonderful gift of teaching the churches to grow as disciples...and he was studious beforehand as well...a devout Jew. When we get saved, when we accept Fatherful...Jesus comes into our lives, our old being dies much like Christ died on the cross, and we rise again as a new being. Most of these gifts we were born with, but until we are born again, we aren't able to use them properly.

In Paul's letter to the Corinthians, he further elaborates on these thoughts mentioning:

> **4 There are different kinds of gifts, but the same Spirit distributes them. 5 There are different kinds of service, but the same Lord. 6 There are different kinds of working, but in all of them and in everyone it is the same God at work. 7 Now to each one the manifestation of the Spirit is given for the common good. 8 To one there is given through the Spirit a message of wisdom, to another a message of knowledge by means of the same Spirit, 9 to another faith by the same Spirit, to another gifts of healing by that one Spirit, 10 to another miraculous powers, to another prophecy, to another distinguishing between spirits, to another speaking in different kinds of tongues, and to still another the interpretation of tongues. 11 All these are the work of one and the same Spirit, and he distributes them to each one, just as he determines.** (1 Corinthians 12:4-11, NIV)

Isn't it exciting to know that you have gifts specific only to you? DNA of spirituality, and useful as such.

I always joke that I am frequently 'picked last for dodgeball', but a famous theologian once said, "the last will be first and the first shall be last" (it was Jesus, Matthew 20:16[33]). Though picked last for dodgeball is something you avoid in worldly life, the Lord used that same act to bring attention to Him choosing me (as choosing you). This last place trophy I typically brought home allowed me to see the good in others; it made me an encourager but also an exhorter. My spiritual gifts have opened the gate to people that most would not have access to, for His kingdom purpose. I am one hundred percent confident, that yours will do the same for you, and you will enjoy the means of employment…and potentially even write a book. I never said, writing was one of my spiritual gifts 😊.

If this sparks your interest, various spiritual gifts tests are available on the internet. It will behoove you to attempt one and discover your own spiritual gifts, as you do this you can feed and flourish them for the kingdom. Keep in mind that these tests are not comprehensive, they are not the Holy Spirit and should be vetted with that in mind. But, if you understand that, you can get a basic idea of which areas you can develop. Copy the link below into your browser to gain more insight.

https://giftstest.com/

---

[33] English Standard Version

Reflections

Use this space to write down what the test stated may be your spiritual gifts. Be open with your test taking aspirations, it's almost like you're meeting a potential part of you that you never knew you had. Enjoy it. Also browse your specific gifts in application.

_____

_____

_____

_____

_____

Open your bible to the following scriptures and write down your observations from the word pertaining to the spiritual gifts:

1 Peter 4:10
Romans 12:4-8
1 Corinthians 12:4-11
1 Corinthians 12:27-30
Ephesians 4:11-16

_____

_____

_____

_____

_____

Were there any gifts that surprised you, and if so why and what were they?

_____

_____

_____

_____

_____

_____

_____

_____

_____

_____

_____

_____

_____

_____

_____

_____

_____

_____

Chapter 15

GRACE UPON GRACE

$\mathcal{B}$ACKPEDAL TO THE BEGINNING OF this book, ensuring you knew 'Fatherful' was not a race, I was sure to indicate that this sort of action happens not all at once...the title maybe so, but the development not so much.

Type-A deadlines, mandates, overperforming, and competition, all are something we're used to (not discrediting these qualities) but it's the opposite of what's required in this journey.

You and God determine your own pace, sometimes life happens and that's okay. God is with you every step of the way. You have been Fatherful since your conception, God chose you before you were born...but because of our focus, due to life events, we couldn't identify that. That's OK! It's alright if you're in your elder years and you're just beginning 'Fatherful', there is no age limit or expiration, come as you are.[34]

As you meditate on these chapters, I want you to make a promise that you will deliver the same grace to yourself and others as God did toward your past. Sometimes we are our worst critics of our own obstacles; don't let the opposer get you like that. You have a toolbox of equipment in your arsenal to move toward becoming 'Fatherful'. It took me twenty-seven years to pick up my life, collect my thoughts

---

[34] Paraphrased Matthew 11:28, ESV

and attempt this testimony; add another four years for life delays. God is just as pleased with *your* initiative and execution as He is through this. Believe in yourself, and trust in your God as He will deliver you out of this desert.

CONTINUED WORD

I thank you for picking up this book and giving it a chance, giving Fatherful a chance… I pray that it has shined a light on something that has been hidden, but most importantly I pray that the Holy Spirit works through the words in this text so that they may bring God glory. I pray that with this, if you have accepted the Lord as your Savior, you are blessed with finding a humble Bible-believing community to hold your hand as you begin to use your spiritual legs. If it ever becomes too difficult to bear, send me an email at fatherlesstofatherful@gmail.com. I will be glad to help and remind you that you are loved and indeed Fatherful. But above all, as you continue upward, put Him first and the rest will fall into place.

"Waking up to a new sunrise
Looking back from the other side
I can see now with open eyes
Darkest water and deepest pain
I wouldn't trade it for anything
Cause my brokenness brought me to You
And these wounds are a story you'll use.[35]"

---

[35] I am They, *Scars,* Essential, Big Future, 2018.

Printed in the United States
by Baker & Taylor Publisher Services